Power Cards:

Using Special Interests to Motivate Children and Youth with Asperger Syndrome and Autism

Power Cards:

Using Special Interests to Motivate Children and Youth with Asperger Syndrome and Autism

Elisa Gagnon

Illustrated by Penny Chiles

AAPC

Autism Asperger Publishing Co.
P.O. Box 23173
Shawnee Mission, Kansas 66283-0173
www.asperger.net

© 2001 by Autism Asperger Publishing Co.
First printing 2001; Second printing 2004
P.O. Box 23173
Shawnee Mission, Kansas 66283-0173
www.asperger.net

Publisher's Cataloging-in-Publication
(Provided by Quality Books, Inc.)

Gagnon, Elisa.
    Power cards : using special interests to motivate
children and youth with Asperger syndrome and autism/
Elisa Gagnon ; illustrator, Penny Chiles -- 1st ed.
    p. cm.
    Includes bibliographical references.
    Library of Congress Control Number: 2001132835
    ISBN 1-931282-01-3

        1. Autistic children--Education--Social aspects.
2. Asperger's syndrome. 3. Autism in children.
4. Motivation in education. I. Title.

LC4717.5.G34 2001   371.94
            QBIO1-700756

This book is designed in Textile and Rotis

Managing Editor: Kirsten McBride
Cover Design: Taku Hagiwara
Production Assistant: Ginny Biddulph
Interior Design/Production: Tappan Design

Printed in the United States of America

*This book is dedicated to the students
in the autism and Asperger Syndrome graduate
program in the Department of Special Education at
the University of Kansas, whose enthusiasm for and
commitment to children and youth with AS is immea-
surable. Their dedication to their profession will
make a difference in the lives of children.*

Table of Contents

After many years of working with children and youth with Asperger Syndrome and autism, it has become clear to me that these students need special supports to meet the challenges at home, school, and in the community. As a teacher I have tried many things, among them visual supports (Hodgdon, 1995; Savner & Myles, 2000); social stories (Gray, 1995; Swaggart, Gagnon, Bock, Earles, Quinn, Myles, & Simpson, 1995); structured classrooms (Schopler & Mesibov, 1995); applied behavior analysis techniques (Leaf & McEachin, 1999; Lovaas, 1987; Simpson & Myles, 1990); joint action routines (Snyder-McLean, Solomonson, McLean, & Sack, 1984); direct instruction (Carnine, 1991); incidental teaching (McGee, Krantz, & McClannahan, 1985); cognitive behavior management techniques (Quinn, Swaggart, & Myles, 1994); social skills programs (Freeman & Dake, 1997; Wilson, 1993); sensory programs (Williams & Shellenberger, 1996); and peer tutoring as well as other peer programs (Kamps, Dugan, Leonard, & Carta, 1990; McGee, Almeida, Sulzer-Azaroff, & Feldman, 1992; Odom & McConnell, 1997).

Although these techniques, either alone or in combination, were successful with many of my students, I still felt that something was missing. I wasn't tapping into the strengths and interests of the children to help them learn and be motivated by learning. Thus, I began using a technique that does just that.

"Claudia's Cards" came out of a sense of desperation when Claudia refused to stay on task; in fact, refused to do anything except sing the theme song from *Sesame Street* and talk about Big Bird. I gained her attention by reading a story I created myself and titled "Big Bird Learns to Stay on Task." After I had her attention, I provided her with a small card with a picture of Big Bird and simple instructions for staying on task. I soon realized that Claudia would do things for Big Bird that she would never consider doing for me. I called the technique "Claudia's Cards" and began using it successfully with other children.

As I used this technique more frequently with other students and saw the positive results, I thought that other teachers and parents might find success with "Claudia's Cards." However, I felt that the technique needed an "official" name that would better describe what it was. After much deliberation, I decided that what I was doing was best described by the term "Power Card Strategy." Briefly, the Power Card Strategy is a visual aid developed by educators and parents to assist students with Asperger Syndrome and autism in making sense of social situations, routines, the meaning of language, and the hidden curriculum that surrounds us wherever we go. What sets the Power Card Strategy apart is that it makes use of children's special interests – one of the unique characteristics of children with autism and AS – to help them make sense of situations they encounter on a daily basis.

A brief scenario is used to explain how the hero or special interest has encountered and solved the problem. Then a POWER CARD (typically the size of a trading card or business card) is created that summarizes the strategy and contains a picture of the special interest. The child carries this card with her as a reminder when similar situations come up.

This book starts out with a discussion of the specific characteristics of Asperger Syndrome and autism that support the use of the Power Card Strategy. Then the strategy and its uses are described in Chapter 2 along with step-by-step directions for creating POWER CARDS. Chapter 3 suggests some novel ways to integrate special interests in a school setting using variations of the Power Card Strategy. Chapter 4 provides samples of how the Power Card Strategy has been used at home, at school in both special education settings and general education classes, and in the community with individuals of varying ages and skill levels. Finally, Chapter 5 reports the results of two classroom studies implementing the Power Card Strategy.

The Power Card Strategy is NOT appropriate for every child with Asperger Syndrome and autism. For example, it may not be appropriate for a child severely impacted with autism, nor may it be appropriate for a child with extremely low motivation. The appropriateness of using the Power Card Strategy, like all teaching techniques, must be evaluated for each individual child.

I hope you meet with the same success that I have enjoyed using the Power Card Strategy.

– Elisa Gagnon

Chapter 1

Characteristics of Asperger Syndrome and Autism That Support the Use of the Power Card Strategy

Hans Asperger's (1944) insightful and detailed descriptions of the children he had seen in his clinical practice was the first formal glimpse of what we have come to know as Asperger Syndrome. The children, he stated, were unique in the cognitive, social and behavioral, language, expressive, and motivational areas. Despite their many challenges, children and youth with this exceptionality had a good prognosis, according to Asperger, because their special interests and unique views would enable them to make meaningful contributions to society and thereby help them gain social acceptance (Frith, 1991), despite challenges in other areas.

Wing's (1981) subsequent discussion of Asperger's work brought this exceptionality to the public's attention. Wing, who conducted several case studies of her own, found a consistency in the characteristics she analyzed and those reported by Asperger some 40 years earlier. Research on Asperger Syndrome has continued since then, and results of these studies have largely supported Asperger's and Wing's work. In 1994, a major landmark in the history of Asperger Syndrome occurred, as the exceptionality became listed in the *Diagnostic and Statistical Manual of Mental Disorders* (4th ed.-Text Revision, DSM-IV-TR; American Psychiatric Association [APA], 2000). This definition appears on the following page.

At about the same time as Asperger reached his conclusions about the children in his clinic, but independently and unknown to him, Kanner (1943) in the United States described a unique group of children whose characteristics made them different from other children with special needs such as those with mental retardation. According to Kanner, these children manifested similar characteristics from infancy or early childhood, including:

- an inability to relate normally to other people and situations

- delayed speech and language development

DSM-IV-TR (2000) Diagnostic Criteria for Asperger Syndrome

A. Qualitative impairment in social interaction, as manifested by at least two of the following:
1. marked impairment in the use of multiple non-verbal behaviors such as eye-to-eye gaze, facial expression, body postures, and gestures to regulate social interaction
2. failure to develop peer relationships appropriate to developmental level
3. a lack of spontaneous seeking to share enjoyment, interests, or achievements with other people (e.g., by a lack of showing, bringing, or pointing out objects of interest to other people)
4. lack of social or emotional reciprocity

B. Restricted repetitive and stereotyped patterns of behavior, interests, and activities as manifested by at least one of the following:
1. encompassing preoccupation with one or more stereotyped and restricted patterns of interest that is abnormal either in intensity or focus
2. apparently inflexible adherence to specific, nonfunctional routines or rituals
3. stereotyped and repetitive motor mannerisms (e.g., hand or finger flapping or twisting, or complex whole-body movements)
4. persistent preoccupation with parts of objects

C. The disturbance causes clinically significant impairment in social, occupational, or other important areas of functioning.

D. There is no clinically significant general delay in language (e.g., single words used by age 2, communication phrases used by age 3 years).

E. There is no clinically significant delay in cognitive development or in the development of age-appropriate self-help skills, adaptive behavior (other than in social interaction), and curiosity about the environment in childhood.

F. Criteria are not met for another specific Pervasive Developmental Disorder or Schizophrenia.

- failure to use developed language for communication purposes and/or other speech and language difficulties, including echolalia, pronoun reversal and misusage and extreme literalness

- normal physical growth and development

- insistence on environmental sameness

- obsessive interest, extreme fascination and preoccupation

- stereotypic, repetitive and other self-stimulatory responses

These characteristics as first described by Kanner have been revised, refined and broadened in recent years. Nonetheless, current definitions of autism continue to reflect many of Kanner's original observations. The DSM-IV definition of autism is provided on page 5.

Currently, it is widely debated whether Asperger Syndrome (AS) and autism are different exceptionalities or whether they occur along a continuum, with AS at the higher-functioning end of the scale.

DSM-IV-TR (2000) Diagnostic Criteria for Autism

A. A total of six (or more) items from (1), (2), and (3), with at least two from (1), and one each from (2) and (3).

  1. qualitative impairment in social interaction, as manifested by at least two of the following:
  - A. marked impairment in the use of multiple nonverbal behaviors such as eye-to-eye gaze, facial expression, body postures, and gestures to regulate social interaction
  - B. failure to develop peer relationships appropriate to developmental level
  - C. a lack of spontaneous seeking to share enjoyment, interests, or achievements with other people (e.g., by a lack of showing, bringing, or pointing out objects of interest)
  - D. lack of social or emotional reciprocity

  2. qualitative impairments in communication as manifested by at least one of the following:
  - A. delay in, or total lack of, the development of spoken language (not accompanied by an attempt to compensate through alternative modes of communication such as gesture or mime)
  - B. in individuals with adequate speech, marked impairment in the ability to initiate or sustain a conversation with others
  - C. stereotyped and repetitive use of language or idiosyncratic language
  - D. lack of varied, spontaneous make-believe play or social imitative play appropriate to developmental level

  3. restricted, repetitive and stereotyped patterns of behavior, interests, and activities, as manifested by at least one of the following:
  - A. encompassing preoccupation with one or more stereotyped and restricted patterns of interest that is abnormal either in intensity or focus
  - B. apparently inflexible adherence to specific, nonfunctional routines or rituals
  - C. stereotyped and repetitive motor mannerisms (e.g., hand or finger flapping or twisting, or complex whole-body movements

B. Delays or abnormal functioning in at least one of the following areas, with onset prior to age 3 years: (1) social interaction, (2) language as used in social communication, or (3) symbolic or imaginative play.

C. The disturbance is not better accounted for by Rett's Disorder or Childhood Disintegrative Disorder.

Regardless of what researchers eventually determine, children we now recognize as having Asperger Syndrome or autism share some of the same characteristics.

This chapter overviews some of the characteristics of these children and youth that make POWER CARDS an effective technique by capitalizing on their special interests and keen visual sense. Specifically, we will discuss the following characteristics:

- IQ
- speech/language
- visual processing
- social skills
- generalization
- failure to understand the hidden curriculum
- special interests
- motivation
- behavior

The vast majority of students with Asperger Syndrome have average to above-average intellectual abilities and are included in general education classrooms.

IQ

The vast majority of students with Asperger Syndrome have average to above-average intellectual abilities and are included in general education classrooms (Barnhill, Hagiwara, Myles, & Simpson, 2000; Ehlers et al., 1997). By comparison, children with autism most often have IQs below 70 (Simpson & Myles, 1998), although many, such as those with high-functioning autism, have higher IQs. Children with AS and autism share several cognitive commonalities, including (a) rote memory, (b) theory-of-mind problems, and (c) problem-solving difficulties.

Rote Memory

Many individuals with AS and autism have well-developed rote memory skills. For example, they can often pick up from conversation or text certain words or phrases and use them in a manner that gives the listener the impression that they comprehend what they are talking about. But this is often misleading.

In fact, rote memory may be a disadvantage for these students. Many educators assume that good rote memory means that students can remember, at any time, pieces of information or events. But this may not be true. While they are storing chunks of information in memory, it is often difficult for individuals with AS or autism to determine how to retrieve this information. They often need a direct "code word" or cue to retrieve information. For example, Deron could list all the food items at McDonald's but could not verbally express what he wanted to order unless the server directly said, "May I take your order?" The question "What would you like?" did not include the code word "order" that Deron needed to retrieve the information.

In other cases, rote memory can be an advantage. Some teachers and parents teach rote memory first and then, once the child knows the rote skill, assign meaning to the skill. For example, when Deron memorized the McDonald's menu he had no idea that it contained names of foods that he would enjoy eating. Making choices had to be taught as a separate skill.

Theory of Mind

Individuals with AS and autism have difficulty understanding how others feel and think. Problems with perspective taking or with viewing a situation from "someone else's standpoint" or "taking a walk in someone else's shoes" are also called theory-of-mind problems. Some think that it is this deficit that sets children with Asperger Syndrome and autism apart from those with other disabilities (Baron-Cohen, 1988; Howlin, Baron-Cohen, & Hadwin, 1999).

A typical theory-of-mind problem is illustrated in the scenario to the right. Other theory-of-mind problems include:

- difficulty explaining own behaviors

- difficulty understanding emotions

- difficulty predicting how others feel or think

- problems understanding the perspectives of others

- problems inferring the intentions of others

- failure to understand that behavior impacts how others think and/or feel

- problems with social conventions such as turn-taking, politeness, and social space

My teacher says I'm rude. I think I'm honest. I don't understand why I can't tell someone that they have bad breath, ugly hair, or to go away because I'm busy.

From *This Is Asperger Syndrome*, by E. Gagnon and B.S. Myles, 1999. Shawnee Mission, KS: AAPC. Reprinted by permission.

Problem Solving

Many children and youth with Asperger Syndrome and autism have difficulty with problem solving as demonstrated by either:

- lacking problem-solving skills

- selecting the wrong problem-solving approach in a given situation

- not knowing when to change from one problem-solving approach to another

Let's look at some examples.

Sarah, a 10-year-old girl with autism, loves to climb. Every day at recess she climbs to the top of the jungle gym where she sits, and sits, and sits. It isn't that she is particularly fond of staying up there, but she simply doesn't have a problem-solving strategy to get down again.

Wu, a 12-year-old boy with Asperger Syndrome, really wants to play basketball with a group of boys in his youth program but he just stands near them and complains about not being asked to play. This is his only problem-solving skill and it is not an effective strategy.

K.C., a child with Asperger Syndrome who has just entered middle school, has difficulty opening his locker. When the combination doesn't work, he just keeps trying over and over again. He doesn't know that after two or three unsuccessful attempts, he should try a different strategy such as asking a teacher or peer for help.

Speech/Language

While individuals with Asperger Syndrome and autism share many language characteristics, they also differ in many respects. For example, nearly all persons with Asperger Syndrome are verbal compared to approximately only half of those with autism. This section focuses on the characteristics shared across the two exceptionalities – social language, abstractions, and choice of words and phrases in expressive language.

Pragmatics - Social Language

Those who are verbal often have good structural language skills, such as clear pronunciation and correct syntax, but poor pragmatic communication abilities. That is, they have difficulty in using language for social reasons. For example, a child may

- repeat the same phrase over and over

- talk with exaggerated inflections or in a monotone and droning style

- discuss at length a single topic that is of little interest to others

- demonstrate difficulty in sustaining conversation unless it focuses exclusively on a particular narrowly defined topic

These communication problems are not surprising, given that effective communication requires that individuals have mutually shared topics to communicate about and are willing to listen as well as to talk – common difficulties for persons with Asperger Syndrome and autism.

Abstractions

Related to school-based interactions, students with Asperger Syndrome and autism frequently experience difficulty comprehending language related to abstract concepts. Understanding and correctly using figures of speech such as metaphors, idioms, parables and allegories and grasping the meaning and intent of rhetorical questions can also cause problems. The illustration to the right shows an example of how idiomatic language can be misinterpreted by individuals with Asperger and autism.

When I walk into the lunch room the kids always say "What's up!" and so I look up. I have a great sense of humor but people seldom get my jokes.

From *This Is Asperger Syndrome*, by E. Gagnon and B.S. Myles, 1999. Shawnee Mission, KS: AAPC. Reprinted by permission.

In another example, Ellen was invited to bring Todd, her 11-year-old son with Asperger Syndrome, to an important meeting in the home of a woman she did not know well. Before entering the woman's house, Ellen went over all the rules she thought Todd needed to remember regarding appropriate behavior. As she rang the doorbell, she thought all was under control. The first half hour or so went well but as Ellen was sitting in the living room during the meeting, she happened to glance into the kitchen where she saw Todd standing on the counter pulling out boxes of cereal from a cabinet. She dashed into the kitchen and asked Todd what he thought he was doing. Todd innocently replied, "It's okay, mom. She told me to make myself at home."

Individuals with Asperger Syndrome and autism also have difficulty understanding abstract concepts such as what is an appropriate topic to be brought up in a given situation, and when and with whom it should be addressed. In the middle of music class one day, Shawn, a 10-year-old boy with Asperger Syndrome, announced in a loud voice, "I have to use the can!" He failed to understand that while this term might be appropriate to use with peers on the playground, it was not appropriate in music class (Gagnon & Myles, 1999).

Choice of Words and Phrases in Expressive Language

The words chosen by a person with Asperger Syndrome or autism to express a sentiment or concept can also lead to miscommunication and misunderstanding. On one occasion, Will greeted a substitute teacher by telling her that she looked exactly like his pet bulldog. The teacher thought Will was being disrespectful and promptly sent him to the

principal's office. After a lengthy and somewhat disconnected discourse, Will managed to explain to the principal that his bulldog was very attractive and that he only was trying to pay the substitute a compliment.

Visual Processing

It has been well documented that children and youth with autism process visual information better than auditory information (Quill, 1995, 2000), and it appears that individuals with Asperger Syndrome share the same characteristics (Barnhill et al., 2000; Dunn, Myles, & Orr, in press). For example, Bock (1994, 1999) successfully taught categorization skills using visual techniques to persons with autism. These skills have generalized to real-life tasks such as restocking shelves in a grocery store and sorting laundry. Although these limited data are not enough on which to base instructional programming, they do support what practitioners have long suspected – to best understand their environment, students with autism and Asperger Syndrome need visual supports.

... to best understand their environment, students with autism and Asperger Syndrome need visual supports.

Social Skills

Social skill problems are often considered one of the hallmark characteristics of children with Asperger Syndrome and autism. On the social continuum, children and youth with AS and autism range from withdrawn to active. However, regardless of where they fall on this continuum, they are routinely viewed as socially awkward and stiff, emotionally blunted, self-centered, unable to understand nonverbal social cues, inflexible, and lacking in empathy and understanding. Therefore, even when children and adolescents with AS and autism actively seek out others, they usually encounter social isolation because of their failure to understand the rules of social behavior, including eye contact, appropriate proximity to others, gestures, posture, and so forth.

Problems Interacting with Others

Not surprisingly, social interaction problems are common. The inability to interact with peers is marked by some of the characteristics that have just been discussed, including

- lack of understanding of social cues

- a tendency to interpret words and/or phrases concretely

- difficulties comprehending abstract language

In addition, persons with AS and autism often exhibit a clumsy social style, engage in one-sided social interactions, and have difficulty accurately sensing the feelings of others or taking others' perspective. Thus, they either monopolize or exhibit no interest in conversation, show abnormalities in inflection, and repeat phrases inappropriately and out of context.

Although individuals with AS and autism are often successful using simple, routine social interactions such as greetings, they may not able to extend this interaction in a meaningful way. When they do attempt to maintain a conversation, it may be marked by language considered inappropriate, such as in the example when Will innocently compared his substitute teacher to a bulldog.

To many persons with AS and autism, conversation exists primarily as a means of talking about a topic that is fascinating to them, regardless of audience input or interest. Without the ability to monitor others' thoughts or value their input, extensive monologues on a restricted topic often occur. They do not understand that when a person rolls her eyes, crosses her arms, or backs away, she is signaling a lack of interest in what the person with AS or autism is saying.

Incidental Social Learning

These difficulties are compounded by the fact that children and youth with AS and autism are often poor incidental social learners. That is, they don't pick up clues from the environment for appropriate behavior and if they learn social skills at all, they often do so without fully understanding their meaning and context. For example, to provide structure to an otherwise confusing world, they attempt to rigidly and broadly follow universal social rules. The movie *Forrest Gump* (Paramount Pictures, 1995) illustrates this tendency well. As a child, Forrest was taught the rule "Never talk to strangers," which he applied faithfully to the bus driver on the first day of school. After the bus driver had introduced

herself to Forrest, he said, "Mama said not to be takin' rides from strangers." Although the bus driver explained that this rule has exceptions, Forrest had to come up with his own strategy before he was comfortable. He proceeded to introduce himself to the bus driver and then stated, "Well, now we ain't strangers any more." Not many students with Asperger Syndrome or autism possess the flexibility of thought to develop a strategy such as this.

Behavior

While behavioral problems are not universal among students with Asperger Syndrome and autism, they are not uncommon. When behavioral difficulties do occur, they typically appear to be a function of:

- social ineptness

- lack of understanding

- high stress level

- lack of control over the environment

- obsessive and single-minded pursuit of a certain interest

- defensive panic reaction

Thus, the behavior problems of children with AS and autism are connected to their more generalized inability to function in a world they perceive to be unpredictable and threatening.

Distractibility and Inattention

Many children and youth with AS and autism share commonalities in terms of distractibility and inattentiveness. Attention often seems fleeting. One moment the student appears to be attending, only the next moment to suddenly withdraw into an inner world and be totally unaware of anything else around her. Teacher directions are not processed; student conversations are not heard. Such daydreaming may occur over extended time periods with no predictability and is often so intense that a physical prompt from the teacher is needed to call the student back to task. Often the cause is unknown, but it may be related to stress, a focus on an obsessive interest, or overstimulation.

Even while attending, the student may not react to teacher instructions. Jason, a 10-year-old student with autism, looked at the teacher when she told the class to get their backpacks and line up. He started to follow this two-step direction but appeared to lose focus right after he got his backpack. As a result, he just stood in the middle of the room until another student prompted him to get in line. Jason was not able to follow this two-step direction and lacked a strategy to ask for assistance.

Students having difficulty following directions may act in a variety of ways. They may remain frozen in the same place, wander aimlessly about, shuffle through their desk, stare into space, or begin to daydream. On rare occasions, they may cause a distraction or act out.

It is generally easier for persons with Asperger Syndrome and autism to function in an organized environment.

Rigidity

Students with Asperger Syndrome typically fall at either end of the continuum of structure: They either have an inherent ability to set up and adhere to a rigid structure or they rely totally on others to help them get organized. Nevertheless, it is generally easier for persons with Asperger Syndrome and autism to function in an organized environment. Therefore, predictable schedules, uniform assignment formats, and consistent teacher affect help these students devote more of their time and energy to academic tasks. Those who have internal structure tend to hold rigid expectations that schedules are followed and commitments are honored. As a result, unscheduled events cause them great discomfort, which can be manifested as disorientation, refusal to engage in a new activity, extended discourse about the canceled or postponed event, or acting out or other behavior problems. In other words, the student communicates through language and behavior that change is difficult.

Irene, a 14-year-old girl with Asperger Syndrome, spends hours arranging and rearranging her bedroom and her backpack. She refuses to go to bed at night until everything is perfect and becomes upset if anyone enters her room uninvited. She lives in constant fear that someone will move something in her room or sit on her bed. If someone touches something in her backpack, she takes everything out and then replaces each item carefully.

On the other end of the continuum, Matthew, a 16-year-old with Asperger Syndrome, relies on others to keep him organized. He functions best in a structured environment but appears to be unable to keep track of clothing, school work, his wallet, or his keys. His mother spends much of her time making sure that Matthew's environment is organized to prevent the inevitable meltdowns that occur if structure is not provided.

Failure to Understand the Hidden Curriculum

An additional characteristic of children and youth with Asperger Syndrome and autism is their difficulty in understanding the hidden curriculum (Myles & Simpson, 1998, 2001; Myles & Southwick, 1999). The "hidden curriculum" can be described as the dos and don'ts of everyday living that are not spelled out or directly taught but that everyone somehow picks up on (Bieber, 1994). For example, one hidden curriculum lesson is that we don't always say what we think. Some parents and teachers have said about children with Asperger Syndrome and autism that "the filter between their child's brain and the mouth is not operating" – the child says exactly what comes to mind. This is often called "blurting." When the individual with Asperger Syndrome or Autism blurts out "Nobody's hair is really that color" or "You smell funny," there is no intention to hurt or make fun; the person is merely stating something as he sees it. Because of incidents like these, people with Asperger Syndrome and autism are commonly described as lacking an awareness of accepted social protocol and common sense.

Margery, a 13-year-old with AS, is a case in point. Most middle school students curse. And even though she is unable to learn appropriate social skills incidentally, Margery has managed to learn from her peers some particularly colorful curse words. Having observed students cursing on the school soccer field, Margery applies the universal rule that cursing is okay outside. However, she has not learned the nuance that you should not curse when the principal is standing beside you. One day when excited during a basketball game, Margery let out a particularly nasty word. Unfortunately, the principal happened to be standing right next to her. Not realizing her transgression, Margery was thrown into a state of confusion when the principal threatened to punish her for what she considered to be a socially appropriate behavior.

LaTonya, an adolescent with autism, learned about menstruation and the related hygiene issues when she started her period, but failed to pick up the more subtle issues surrounding this developmental milestone. Everyone in the general education home economics class was surprised one day when LaTonya suddenly exclaimed loudly, "I need to change my pad." Her parents and teachers had failed to teach her that it was not appropriate to announce this openly to the entire class.

It is a virtually impossible task to identify all hidden curriculum items. They vary by age, environment, culture, and social circumstances. An abbreviated list of hidden curriculum items appears below.

Sample Hidden Curriculum Items

BATHROOM

1. Don't write on the bathroom walls, especially when there is an adult in the bathroom.

2. For boys, don't talk to others in a restroom while you are urinating.

3. For girls, know which toilets you can sit on and which ones you should squat over.

SCHOOL

1. Don't bring tuna fish to school in your lunch – it smells and kids won't want to sit by you.

2. When walking up/down staircases, stay on the right so you are not walking against the traffic.

3. Don't look over someone's shoulder when he/she is checking e-mail.

4. When a teacher gives you a warning about a behavior and you continue that behavior, you are probably going to get into trouble.

5. When you are taking a shower in gym class, do not sustain eye contact for very long or watch others take their showers.

6. Do not pass gas, pick your nose, or scratch an itch of a private body part in any class.

7. Talk to teachers using a pleasant tone of voice because they will respond to you in a more positive manner. They also like it if you smile every once in a while.

8. Rules change from teacher to teacher and it does not do any good to focus on the fact that it may not be fair.

9. When a teacher tells a student to stop talking, it is not a good idea to start talking to your neighbor since the teacher has already expressed disapproval of that action.

10. If you do something funny, it is usually only funny once. If you do it repeatedly, it makes you look silly and goofy and people might make fun of you.

Special Interests

Special interests are evidenced in both individuals with Asperger Syndrome and autism. Interests, which are most often narrowly focused, can be (a) tangible, such as collecting rocks made of mica or automobile hood ornaments; or (b) topical, such as knowing everything about the Civil War or upright vacuum cleaners. These special interests can be age appropriate. But "Even when these interests appear to be age appropriate, as for

example in sport or computers, they can be become so intense and overwhelming that they effectively prevent the child taking part in other activity" (Howlin, 1998, p. 14). Some use their special interest to gain positive attention. Melvin, who knows all the facts about dinosaurs, is considered a dinosaur expert at his school. Steven, who knows about baseball, was asked to be in the school's Quiz Bowl in which sports questions often dominate.

Recent studies include the work of Baker, Koegel, and Koegel (1998), who found that including the use of special interests increased willingness to participate, and resulted in an increase of appropriate social skills. An additional study by Baker (2000) suggested that incorporating special interests into play increased social interactions between those with autism and their siblings. Mercier, Mottron, and Belleville (2000) interviewed people with autism about their special interests and concluded that special interests are highly reinforcing. The interview questions related to the content and expression of their special interest and also included questions about the reaction of others to the special interest.

... performance improved when special interests were used as reinforcers.

Further, Charlop-Christy and Haynes (1998) assessed the effectiveness of special interests as reinforcers to improve task performance in children with autism. The study showed that performance improved when special interests were used as reinforcers. Hinton and Kern (1999) incorporated the special interests of students with behavior disorders to increase homework completion. After incorporating student interests, homework completion increased dramatically. Sugai and White (1986) used special interests to decrease undesired behavior in an adolescent with autism. The 13-year-old boy's interest in object stimulation was used to decrease off-task behavior in prevocational tasks. This also proved to be successful.

Motivation

Students with Asperger Syndrome and autism are often difficult to motivate. They may be withdrawn, uninterested in exploring new environments, or preoccupied with obsessive interests. These special interests may be the key to motivation. Jeffrey, a 10-year-old with Asperger Syndrome, has difficulty learning math facts, staring off into space when math is introduced in group or individual settings. He continually attempts to change math-related conversation to his obsession – the World Wrestling Federation. He became motivated to work on math when his teacher added a wrestling theme to his math instruction. Briefly, Jeffrey's teacher gave each numeral a wrestling personality and turned word problems into wrestling matches.

According to Olly (1992), "One of the most commonly heard comments about people with autism is that they are not motivated to engage in education or treatment programs" (p. 11). Although individuals with Asperger Syndrome and autism appear to have low motivation, the truth is that they often have a different type of motivation (Baker, 2000; Dunlap, Foster-Johnson, Clarke, Kern, & Childs, 1995; Sugai & White, 1986). And until teachers and parents find out what the motivator is, it is difficult to prompt the student to complete work and related tasks.

Generalization

A challenge facing children and youth with Asperger Syndrome and autism relates to their difficulty in generalizing knowledge and skills. That is, they frequently have problems applying information and skills across settings and with different individuals as well as integrating learned material and experience. While some students memorize sets of facts, these lists often remain unconnected bits of information. For example, a student may be able to cite a rule or set of procedures she is supposed to follow in a given situation, but be incapable of applying them when needed. Teachers often voice concern over this lack of generalization, misinterpreting the lack of symmetry between verbalization and actions as intentional misbehavior.

Fernando had learned everything he knew about restaurants from his visits to McDonald's, so the first time he went to a "real sit-down restaurant" he looked for the line to stand in to order his food. Staring in all directions, he finally saw the waitress leaving the kitchen with a tray of food and mistakenly thought the line was behind the kitchen door. When his mother noticed he was missing, Fernando had already gone into the kitchen and given his order to the chef.

This situation is typical for many individuals with Asperger Syndrome and autism. Generalization problems may occur because they have problems retrieving learned behavior from the area of the brain in which it is "filed" for future reference and difficulty "reading" and "interpreting" social clues received from the environment.

Individuals with autism and Asperger Syndrome see the world differently than others do. They are visual learners who require interventions that can tap into their strengths and interests. The Power Card Strategy discussed in the following chapters is designed to do just that.

Special thanks to Brenda Smith Myles for sharing her stories.

Chapter 2

Developing and Using the Power Card Strategy

The Power Card Strategy is a visual aid that incorporates the child's special interest in teaching appropriate social interactions including routines, behavior expectations, the meaning of language, and the hidden curriculum. As mentioned in Chapter 1, the Power Card Strategy is effective because it takes into account the unique characteristics of children and youth with Asperger Syndrome and autism.

Briefly, the Power Card Strategy consists of presenting on a single sheet or in booklet form a short scenario, written in the first person, describing how the child's hero solves a problem and a small card, the POWER CARD, which recaps how the child can use the same strategy to solve a similar problem herself.

The hero or special interest serves several purposes:

1. The underlying purpose is to serve as a motivator. Students with Asperger Syndrome and autism most often "tune in" when their special interest is mentioned.

2. Using the special interest is nonthreatening. Individuals with Asperger Syndrome and autism often find it easier to buy into this sort of scenario than follow a top-down command of "Here is what you have to do."

3. The Power Card Strategy capitalizes on the "relationship" between the child and the hero or role model. Since the child wants to be like his hero, he is more likely to do what the hero suggests.

Grant has difficulty greeting people. Specifically, he tends to avoid eye contact and after shaking a person's hand refuses to let go of it after a suitable length of time. Grant's special interest is the television game show *Who Wants to Be a Millionaire* hosted by Regis Philbin. Following the basic principles behind the Power Card Strategy, the scenario about Grant's special interest and the target behavior follows.

1. Look at the person's eyes when you are greeting them.
2. Say "Hi."
3. Extend your right hand to shake their right hand.
4. Use an up-and-down motion.
5. Count to four in your head when shaking their hand and then let go.

Regis Greets His Contestants
by Cindy Van Horn

Regis Philbin enjoys being the host of "Who Wants to Be a Millionaire," because it gives him a chance to meet and greet new people. When Regis greets a new contestant, he shakes their hand and says "Hi." Regis knows that it is important when shaking a contestant's hand to look at the contestant's eyes so they know he is talking to them. This makes the contestant feel happy. Regis also counts to four in his head when shaking their hand and then lets go of their hand so they can sit down and begin the game.

Regis wants everyone to know that greeting someone correctly makes the person you are greeting happy. He wants you to remember these five steps when greeting someone:

1. Look at the person's eyes when you are greeting them.

2. Say "Hi."

3. Extend your right hand to shake their right hand.

4. Use an up-and-down motion.

5. Count to four in your head when shaking their hand and then let go.

Remember to follow Regis' five steps and others will enjoy meeting and greeting you!

In the first paragraph, Grant discovers that his hero, Regis, places value on the ability to greet people appropriately.

The second paragraph encourages Grant to attempt the new behavior – in this case, greeting someone appropriately – and the behavior is broken down into manageable steps. Grant was encouraged to practice the replacement behavior several times and was verbally praised for "greeting appropriately, just like Regis."

After Grant was introduced to the scenario, he was given the POWER CARD. About the size of a business card, the POWER CARD consists of a picture related to Regis Philbin's show and the steps that Grant needs to remember when greeting people.

What Are the Components of the Power Card Strategy?

To be effective, the Power Card Strategy must include the elements just illustrated in Grant's case.

1. A *brief scenario* using the student's hero or special interest and the behavior or situation that is difficult for the child or youth. The scenario is written at the individual's comprehension level. For example, a scenario for a high school student with Asperger Syndrome might be written on a single page in paragraph form. For an elementary student with autism, it might be written in a large font using several pages with pictures of the special interest throughout. Relevant pictures or graphics include magazine pictures, computer-generated photographs downloaded from the Internet, teacher drawings, student drawings, or icons.

   In the first paragraph, the hero or role model attempts a solution to the problem and experiences success. The second paragraph encourages the student to try out the new behavior, which is broken down into three to five manageable steps.

2. The *POWER CARD* is the size of a trading card, bookmark, or business card. It contains a small picture of the special interest and the solutions to the problem behavior or situation broken down into three to five steps. The POWER CARD is provided to aid in generalization. It can be carried in a purse, wallet or pocket or it can be velcroed inside a book, notebook, or locker. It may also be placed on the corner of a student's desk.

Where Can the Power Card Strategy Be Used?

The Power Card Strategy is appropriate for behaviors or situations in which:

1. The student lacks understanding of what she is to do, such as hidden curriculum items, routines, or language use that the student has not been taught.

2. The student does not understand that he has choices.

3. The student has difficulty understanding that there is a cause-and-effect relationship between a specific behavior and its consequence.

4. The student has difficulty remembering what to do without a prompt.

5. The student does not understand the perspective of others.

6. The student knows what to do when calm but cannot follow a given routine under stress.

7. The student needs a visual reminder to recall the behavioral expectation for a situation.

8. The student has difficulty generalizing.

9. The student is difficult to motivate and may be motivated only by the special interest.

10. The student has difficulty accepting directions from an adult.

For any strategy to be effective, it is important to consider the individual needs of the child and create a plan accordingly.

The Power Card Strategy is usually NOT appropriate when:

1. The student has sensory needs such as difficulty tolerating certain noises, smells or tastes. Although the strategy can help students realize that they may be experiencing a need for sensory input, it alone will not satisfy that need. The strategy may serve as a slight delay, however, by reminding the child what she needs to do to get her needs met.

2. The child is extremely challenged cognitively and appears not to understand spoken language at the sentence or paragraph level. To use the Power Card Strategy, the child does not have to be a reader if pictures or graphics are used to explain the problem situation or behavior and the teacher serves as the reader.

3. The student engages in the problem behavior only once. It is difficult to determine a cause or motivation for a behavior unless it occurs somewhat frequently.

4. The teacher or other adults do not have a positive relationship with the child. Remember, the Power Card Strategy is not a punishment. It should not be perceived as negative in any way. It is fulfilling a need for the child while capitalizing on his special interest.

5. The child is in crisis. When the child is in the rage stage (Myles & Southwick, 1999), this technique will not work. Since the child is not functioning at his optimal level, he cannot make rational decisions. Worse, yet, using the Power Card Strategy at the rage stage will make this technique less effective at times when it is otherwise appropriate.

6. The child does not have a well-developed area of interest. In order to buy into the strategy, the child needs to want to follow the hero's directions.

What Are the Steps in Using the Power Card Strategy?

For any strategy to be effective, it is important to consider the individual needs of the child and create a plan accordingly. Sometimes, a teacher or parent will say, "I tried that and it didn't work," when in reality very little time was invested in developing and carrying out the plan. The following steps are suggested to ensure optimal success.

1. **Identify the problem behavior or situation.** The educator or parent must identify the behavior or situation and state it clearly. It is important to address only one behavior at a time.

2. **Identify the child's special interest.** In many cases, an area of interest is already obvious. If not, consider using a reinforcement survey or converse with the child or youth to determine an area of interest.

3. **Conduct a functional assessment.** The purpose of a functional assessment is to determine the reason or trigger for a particular problem behavior. Researchers and practitioners have developed a list of possible behavior functions or triggers, which include (a) escape/avoidance; (b) attention from peers or adults; (c) expression of anger or stress; (d) emotional state such as depression, frustration and confusion; (e) power control; (f) intimidation; (g) sensory stimulation; (h) fear or relief of fear; (i) request to obtain something – such as food, activity, object, comfort, routine, social interaction; or (j) expression of internal stimulation (i.e., sinus pain, skin irritation, hunger). Other triggers commonly found among children and youth with Asperger Syndrome and autism include (a) obsessional thoughts, (b) fear of failure, (c) fear related to self-esteem, and (d) lack of understanding behavioral expectations, routines, or commands (Myles & Southwick, 1999).

    School personnel may elect to use one of many commercially developed functional assessment instruments, including the *Motivation Assessment Scale* (Durand & Crimmins, 1992) or the *Student-Assisted Functional Assessment Interview* (Kern, Dunlap, Clarke, & Childs, 1994). Many school districts develop their own instruments, which take into account their school environment and culture as well as the special characteristics of children and youth with Asperger Syndrome and autism.

4. **Determine whether the Power Card Strategy is an appropriate intervention.** As mentioned earlier, there are many situations in which the Power Card Strategy will work and many behavioral functions for which it is effective. However, there are just as many situations and functions for which it will not work. Therefore, determining whether the Power Card Strategy is an appropriate intervention is an important step. Sometimes, on the surface, this strategy may not appear to be the best intervention; however, a closer analysis will reveal that it would indeed help the student. For example, if a child with Asperger Syndrome loses control because of stress and anxiety, the strategy will not relieve that stress. However, the Power Card Strategy can help prompt the student to get to a safe place to de-stress or get sensory input, if that is what the child needs. Similarly, if a student with autism wants to escape/avoid the lunchroom, the Power Card Strategy will probably not reduce that desire or need. However, it can provide him with an alternative and an acceptable way to meet this need. In this case, the strategy could prompt the child to ask the lunch attendant for permission to take his lunch to the resource room to eat with a small group.

5. **Collect baseline data.** Collecting data over several days enables educators to determine a pattern of behavior. Baseline data collection typically spans three to five days but in some cases it could be longer to ensure that enough appropriate information has been gathered. No elaborate system is required. A behavior may be measured by simply placing tally marks on a sheet of paper each time the behavior occurs or by using a stopwatch to record the length of time a behavior occurs.

6. **Write the scenario and design the POWER CARD.** The scenario and the POWER CARD should be written in accordance with the student's comprehension skills, using vocabulary and print size that has been individualized for each student. The scenario is written in the first person and either in the present (to describe a situation as it occurs) or the future tense (to anticipate an upcoming event). The first paragraph of the scenario relates to the "hero" or special interest, followed by a section that provides a solution to the problem. This solution is then applied to the child or youth's particular situation.

Decisions on when to fade the scenario will vary based on students' individual needs. It is better to fade too late than too early.

7. **Introduce the scenario and POWER CARD to the child.** Before writing the scenario and POWER CARD, the teacher who has a positive rapport with the student discusses how the Power Card Strategy works in general and how it will work with the student. After the scenario and POWER CARD are written, the teacher or student read it together. This initial read-through should be followed by a discussion. Further, the student who is able to read independently should be encouraged to read the scenario and POWER CARD to other significant adults or peers so that everybody has a similar perspective of the problem situation and appropriate behaviors.

8. **Collect intervention data to determine effectiveness.** Data should be collected throughout the intervention process using the same procedures that were used to gather baseline data.

9. **Evaluate the intervention and make modifications, if needed.** If the desired changes fail to occur after implementing the intervention for two weeks, review the scenario and POWER CARD and the implementation procedures. If alterations are made, it is recommended that only one variable is changed at a time. For example, start by changing the content of the scenario, rather than simultaneously also changing the time when the scenario is read *and* the person who reads it. By changing only one factor at a time, the adult can determine the factor or factors that best facilitate learning.

10. **Empower the student to determine how long to keep using the Power Card Strategy.** Frequent verbal reinforcement will help the child or youth understand that she has the skills necessary to maintain the appropriate behavior. When the child or youth internalizes the appropriate response, she is ready to perform the skill on a consistent basis.

11. **Based on student input and performance, fade reading of the scenario while still keeping the POWER CARD.** Decisions on when to fade the scenario will vary based on students' individual needs. It is better to fade too late than too early. In fact, we recommend that the student be given the control in determining when a given scenario is no longer needed.

12. **Based on student input and performance, fade the use of POWER CARD.** Again, students should be empowered to decide when and if to fade the POWER CARD. Too often we are tempted to pull back on the use of the POWER CARD when we see the youth being successful. Remember, the child is being successful because she has learned how to use the POWER CARD. Therefore, careful consideration must be given before removing it.

NOTE. *It is possible that the student will want to retain the POWER CARD, even though she refers to it infrequently. This should be allowed and even encouraged, if the student perceives it as providing support.*

Can the Power Card Strategy Be Used at Home?

Yes, the Power Card Strategy can be used at home. But chances are that all 12 steps just outlined are not necessary at home. Since parents are familiar with their child's special interest and needs, deciding how to use the strategy is easier.

Some questions to ask when selecting a behavior for change are:

1. Will the Power Card Strategy make a significant difference in my child's and my family's life?

2. Will this make my child feel better about herself?

3. Will the strategy give my child independence?

4. Is it important to my child and my family that this behavior be addressed?

If parents answer "yes" to any of these questions, the behavior is probably one that should be addressed by this strategy or some other method.

The components of the Power Card Strategy were presented earlier. While some parents may produce sophisticated computer-generated scenarios and POWER CARDS, we have found that the strategy is also effective when handwritten. Parents and their children can cut pictures from magazines, take photographs, download images from the Internet, or draw a special interest. The POWER CARD can be cut from construction paper or file folder material. One parent whose child's special interest was Batman photographed her son at Halloween in his Batman costume and used that picture on both the scenario and the POWER CARD.

Once you try the Power Card Strategy, how do you know if it works? Maybe there are changes in your child or you, such as:

1. Is your child tantrumming less often? Children often tantrum because they do not know how to do something or how to get their needs met. The strategy may help the child understand or get something he needs.

2. Have you noticed that your child has learned new and more positive behaviors?

3. Do you as a parent feel less stressed?

4. Does it feel easier to be at home and to go out in the community with your son or daughter (Savner & Myles, 2000)?

Summary

The Power Card Strategy is a technique that may help children and youth with Asperger Syndrome and autism function more appropriately and more comfortably at school, home, and in the community. By using a special interest, the child is motivated to use the strategy presented in the scenario and on the POWER CARD. Generalization is programmed through the POWER CARD to ensure that the identified behavior does not occur in just one environment. This positive strategy is often entertaining for the child and is inexpensive and relatively simple to develop. The Power Card Strategy can make a difference in the lives of many individuals with Asperger Syndrome and autism and those who teach them and love them.

Chapter 3

Using the Power Card Strategy and Special Interests to Increase Academic Performance

with Kathy Wadman

Variations of the Power Card Strategy can be used in multiple ways. For example, the strategy can be used as a basis for a modified curriculum for students with Asperger Syndrome and autism. In fact, without the Power Card Strategy these students may not make academic progress commensurate with their potential.

For example, Andrew, a 10-year-old with a diagnosis of Asperger Syndrome, has a special interest in law enforcement but is discouraged from discussing this at school because both his teacher and his parents fear that by being so focused on this one topic, he will not be able to complete his assignments. Andrew spends his days thinking about law enforcement and although he is reprimanded each time he brings up the subject, he doesn't stop daydreaming about cops and robbers or replaying police movies in his mind. Andrew seldom completes assignments and has no friends. Despite an above-average IQ, his grades are well below average and getting him to attend school is a daily struggle.

Andrew is also difficult to motivate. Typically, he does not respond to the kinds of reinforcement systems that are effective for other students in his class. For example, Miss Newman gives extra minutes of recess when students complete assignments in a timely fashion. The rest of the class loves this incentive, but Andrew hates recess and does everything he can think of to sabotage other students so they won't get extra time on the playground. Needless to say, such behavior further alienates him from his peers.

Andrew is typical of many children with AS in that his area of interest is obvious. However, this is not the case with everybody. In those instances where an area of interest is not easily identified, there are three primary ways to obtain this information: (a) by observing the student during unstructured time (i.e., free-choice time, play time, recess, break time); (b) through informal conversation with the student; or (c) by completion of an interest inventory or reinforcement survey (see Chapter 2).

Once the area of interest is determined, it is beneficial for those who work with the student to brainstorm ways to incorporate the area of interest into the curriculum and all other aspects of the school day. Throughout this process, it is important for the team to consider the special interest as a strength that can be used to the child's benefit rather than to view it as a liability that needs to be eliminated. This is not to say that the student should be allowed to spend all of his time obsessing about his interest. Rather, the special interest is used to spark an interest in curriculum, encourage task completion, and improve behavior. As with all interventions, it is important to collect data to determine the success of the intervention.

In the rest of this chapter we will look at specific youngsters with AS and autism and analyze how their special interests were turned into an asset to improve their academic performance.

... without the Power Card Strategy these students may not make academic progress commensurate with their potential.

Kyle

Kyle is a delightful eight-year-old with a diagnosis of autism. Kyle spends part of his school day in a special education resource room and the remainder of the time in a second-grade general education classroom. His services include paraeducator support in the general education classroom, as needed, and direct instruction in the resource room for math, written language, and reading.

Developing curriculum for Kyle proved difficult initially. His short attention span and limited verbal language made it almost impossible to measure his reading comprehension. In addition, his apparent lack of interest in anything academic compounded the situation. However, it was determined that Kyle had a strong interest in dogs as he often mentioned his dog, Fly. As a result, he was encouraged to talk about his dog with those who worked with him during social skills training as well as during unstructured time. Gradually, it became clear that using this topic could be key to Kyle's academic and social success.

As a result, the following tasks were incorporated into Kyle's day:

1. ***Encourage Kyle to ask others about their dogs***. This became Kyle's way to initiate conversation with adults and peers. At first Kyle would ask, "Do you have a dog?" Later this was expanded to asking specific questions about the dog such as "What type of dog do you have?," "What color is your dog?," and so on. A POWER CARD provided visual support by reminding Kyle of appropriate questions he could ask.

2. ***Create a picture book of different dogs.***
As a start, pictures of dogs were cut out of magazines or downloaded from the Internet. Soon, those who knew Kyle brought photographs of their dogs to be included in the picture book. Kyle also added written text to the picture book describing the dogs, thereby providing handwriting and keyboarding practice. Further, Kyle looked at the picture book with adults and peers during free time and used the pictures to initiate conversation. Finally, the picture book was used as a reinforcer – Kyle was motivated to complete assignments so he could look at the picture book.

3. ***Adapt Kyle's curriculum to incorporate his interest in dogs.***
Whenever possible, Kyle's curriculum was modified to include his area of interest. For example, math word problems included references to dogs and reading included stories about dogs.

Encouraging Kyle's interest in dogs allowed him the opportunity to make academic gains, increased his time on task and improved his ability to communicate. It also improved his social status among his peers, as the other second graders regarded Kyle as "the expert on dogs."

The Power Card Strategy can be used as a basis for a modified curriculum for students with AS and autism.

Jeffrey

Jeffrey, a third grader with a diagnosis of Asperger Syndrome, spends the majority of his school day in a third-grade classroom. His learning opportunities are hindered by distractibility, lack of sustained attention, and disorganization. Difficulties in gross- and fine-motor tasks further complicated his school day, particularly when he was required to complete written assignments or expected to participate in organized large-group activities in physical education or at recess.

Math and written language were especially challenging for Jeffrey. In math, he experienced difficulty with number recall and computation. In written language he tended to stray off the topic or became lost in his thoughts and constant daydreaming.

Through observation his resource room teacher determined that Jeffrey was very interested in the World Wrestling Federation and also in a variety of imaginary characters he created related to wrestling. Despite these interests, however, Jeffrey had poor social skills and was unable to connect with his peers.

The following modifications were provided for Jeffrey:

1. ***Incorporate World Wrestling Federation (WWF) characters into Jeffrey's math lessons***. Jeffrey and his teacher assigned a wrestler to each numeral (for example, Kane was number 7 and The Rock was number 8) and Jeffrey created a story for each math fact. When recalling the sum of 7 x 8, Jeffrey would recall the story he had created as well as the math fact. Although this appeared complex to his teacher, it was an excellent memory aid for Jeffrey. His motivation increased and he was eager to create new vignettes.

2. ***Incorporate WWF into the algorithm of double-digit multiplication.*** Jeffrey experienced difficulty with recall until double-digit multiplication became a tag team wrestling bout. For example, the problem 55 x 32 became the "five" brothers against the team of "three and two."

3. ***Use the WWF characters to "breathe life" into story problems.*** It was easy to change names in story problems to those of members of the WWF. This simple strategy made a remarkable difference in motivation.

4. ***Allow Jeffrey to incorporate wrestling characters into creative writing projects and research projects.*** For example, the make-believe wrestling character "Doink" became the epitome of the Florida tourist in his research paper on "The Animals of Florida."

5. ***Use the Power Card Strategy to address Jeffrey's social skill concerns.*** The scenario and POWER CARD developed for Jeffrey used WWF characters and provided information related to initiating and sustaining a conversation.

Adapted from *Social Skills Training: Practical Solutions for Students with Asperger Syndrome, High-Functioning Autism, and Related Social Communication Disorders,* by Jed Baker, in press. Shawnee Mission, KS: AAPC. Reprinted with permission.

Incorporating special interests into his school day decreased Jeffrey's stress level and enabled him to focus on academic topics. In addition, other students began to view Jeffrey as an intelligent and highly original thinker. As peers began to see him in a positive light, Jeffrey's self-esteem improved.

Matt

Matt, a first grader with a diagnosis of Asperger Syndrome, has a near-obsessive interest in fairy-tales. He is making little academic progress. By January of his first-grade year, Matt is already behind his peers in reading and his classroom teacher considers him a nonreader. Like many children with Asperger Syndrome, Matt does not have the emotional resources to cope with classroom demands, is easily stressed, and cannot tolerate making mistakes. Not surprisingly, his behavioral outbursts, off-task behavior, and noncompliance interfere with his ability to learn. His teachers can almost always predict when a meltdown is about to occur because Matt starts rubbing his hands on his jeans. At the end of the day he receives help in the special education resource room. However, by that time he is overwhelmed and exhausted, making this a less than optimal time for instruction.

The following modifications were provided for Matt:

1. *Use the Power Card Strategy to address Matt's stress and frustration.* Matt, whose interest in fairy-tales included *Jack and the Beanstalk*, became more focused in the classroom when presented with a POWER CARD featuring "Jack."

When Jack begins to rub his hands on his jeans, he knows he can:
- Go to home base.
- Ask his teacher for help.
- Go get a drink of water.
I can also do these things when I rub my hands on my jeans!

2. *Provide Matt the opportunity to dictate fairy-tales.* A variation of a language experience approach was used, which provided Matt the opportunity to dictate stories to his teacher. Matt added illustrations and was anxious to "read" the completed story to his teacher.

Once the topical interest was incorporated, he demonstrated a remarkable ability to recall words. Phonics instruction was added at a later date and Matt currently reads above grade level.

3. ***Allow Matt to use reading as a free-time activity.*** Since Matt often chose solitary activities and peer interactions were limited, providing him with preferred reading material proved to be calming to him. On occasion, Matt would read fairy-tales with other children in the class.

4. ***Allow Matt to draw during instructional time.*** At first glance, it appeared that Matt was not paying attention to what was going on around him while he was drawing, but in reality his comprehension improved when he was permitted to draw. Not surprisingly, his drawings always reflected his topical interest.

5. ***Allow Matt to choose topics for written work.*** Simply allowing Matt to choose his topic reduced frustration and refusals to work. This, in turn, reduced power struggles and confrontations and the quality of his work improved.

6. ***Modify Matt's school day so as to schedule time in the resource room early in the day.*** Matt was able to focus early in the morning and was more likely to work up to his potential.

... Using an area of interest is often the key to improved behavior and academic success.

Summary

Creative educators know the value of tapping into students' strengths. Many children with Asperger Syndrome and autism are difficult to motivate, but using an area of interest is often the key to improved behavior and academic success. Whether using the Power Card Strategy, adapting curriculum to reflect the interest of the child, or a combination of both, using a special interest is a low-cost, effective positive behavioral support.

Chapter 4

Power Card Strategy Samples

This chapter contains scenarios and POWER CARDS that have been used with children and youth with Asperger Syndrome and autism. Each example briefly describes a child or youth, his or her special interest, a target behavior, and the Power Card Strategy used to meet the student's needs.

The POWER CARD samples in this chapter include photos, line drawings, material downloaded from the Internet, etc. This is done to illustrate the range of materials that may be used so long as the child's special interest or other motivator is featured prominently.

Bryan

Bryan is a seven-year-old with high-functioning autism. Bryan's mother struggled to get Bryan to wear a seatbelt and had to physically buckle him in because he refused to do it himself. Using the characters of Bryan's favorite television show, *The Brady Bunch*, his parents designed a POWER CARD and the accompanying scenario to teach him to buckle up independently.

The Brady Bunch Click

by Cindy Van Horn

The Brady children know that before their mother starts the car they have to put on a seatbelt. Greg, Marcia, Peter, Jan, Bobby and Cindy all know that wearing their seatbelt in the car keeps them safe in case their car is in an accident or if the car has to stop quickly. With six children in the family, Mrs. Brady cannot help each child put their seatbelt on, so they had to learn how to do it on their own. When they hear the "click" of the seatbelt, it makes them feel happy because they know that they will be safe. Now when they ride in their friend's car, they can buckle their own seatbelt and do not have to ask for help.

The Brady children want you to be safe when you ride in the car. They know that you too can buckle your own seatbelt if you follow these steps:

1. Grip the buckle with one hand and the seatbelt with the other.

2. Pull the seatbelt to the buckle.

3. Push the seatbelt clip into the buckle until you hear a "click."

The Brady children love to go places and know that the only way they get there is in the car. They know how important it is to be safe, so they always wear their seatbelts. Greg, Marcia, Peter, Jan, Cindy and Bobby want you to be safe too, so "Please, make it CLICK!"

(Card illustration)
1. Grip the buckle with one hand and the seatbelt with the other.
2. Pull the seatbelt to the buckle.
3. Push the seatbelt clip into the buckle until you hear a "click."

This scenario was more effective in a booklet form with illustrations because Bryan is a beginning reader and enjoys picture books.

Jeremy

Jeremy, a nine-year-old with high-functioning autism, often refuses to go to bed at night, leaving him exhausted at school the next day. His parents feel they have tried everything. Jeremy's classroom teacher has arranged for Jeremy to e-mail a local fireman on a regular basis after he has completed academic tasks at school. This has proven to be a powerful reinforcer for Jeremy, who has a huge interest in firefighting and often talks about becoming a fireman when he grows up.

Using the following scenario and POWER CARD helped Jeremy understand the importance of a full night's sleep and consequently helped him go to bed without a struggle. He even took his POWER CARD to bed with him at night.

(Card illustration)
1. Follow a bedtime routine. Fireman Steve takes a bath, brushes his teeth, and reads for 15 minutes before turning off the light.
2. Close your eyes and try to lie still.
3. Stay in bed after the lights are out.

Fireman Steve Goes to Bed

by Nicole Rahaim

Fireman Steve really enjoys being a fireman. Sometimes he gets back to the firehouse after a fire and has trouble going to sleep. He thinks that it might be more fun to stay up and watch television or talk with the other firemen but he knows he needs his sleep. He knows that it is important to get a good night's sleep so he will be rested and do a good job when there is another fire.

It is important for all future firefighters to learn to get a good night's sleep when they are young. Fireman Steve has learned to do these three things when he has trouble going to bed:

1. Follow a bedtime routine. Fireman Steve takes a bath, brushes his teeth, and reads for 15 minutes before turning off the light.

2. Close your eyes and try to lie still.

3. Stay in bed after the lights are out.

Fireman Steve is proud of young men who get plenty of rest every night. He knows that they will make great firefighters some day!

Suzy

Suzy is a 12-year-old girl with a diagnosis of Asperger Syndrome who frequently uses inappropriate and assaulting language with her peers. She continually says exactly what is on her mind with comments such as "You have bad breath" or "Your hair looks terrible today." It is especially difficult for Suzy to be nice to people when she is tired or under stress. When her parents or teachers discuss this with her, she gets defensive and argues that she is merely telling the truth or that she is tired and shouldn't have to be nice to people when she is tired. She fails to see the connection between her lack of friends and the way she speaks to others.

Suzy is a fan of Britney Spears and enjoys her music. Using the following scenario and POWER CARD decreased the occurrence of rude comments Suzy made to others.

1. Think before you say anything. Say it in your head first before saying it out loud.

2. If you can't think of something nice to say, don't say anything.

3. You do not have to say every thought out loud that you think.

Britney and Her Fans
by Cassie Jones

Britney Spears loves being a music star, but sometimes it is difficult for her to be nice to everyone. At the end of a long day in the recording studio or after a concert, she is often tired and it is difficult for her to be nice to her fans and friends. But Britney has learned that it is important to smile at people she meets and say nice things to everyone even when she is tired. She has learned that if she can't say something nice, it is better to just smile and say nothing at all. She stops and thinks about comments she makes before she says anything.

Just like Britney, it is important for young people to think before they talk. It makes Britney proud when preteens and teenagers remember to do the following:

1. Think before you say anything. Say it in your head first before saying it out loud.

2. If you can't think of something nice to say, don't say anything.

3. You do not have to say every thought out loud that you think.

1. Put the cap on the end of your marker before you draw.

2. Be careful to only draw on the paper.

3. Put the cap back on the marker when you are finished.

Meghan

Meghan is an eight-year-old girl with autism. After she completes her assignments, she loves drawing with markers on a piece of butcher paper. Unfortunately, she sometimes draws on the table as well as on her body and is constantly losing the caps of her markers. Meghan has a special interest in Barbie, often carrying her doll with her. She also enjoys discussing Barbie merchandise and looking at picture books with Barbie themes. The following scenario and POWER CARD were written to encourage Meghan to use markers appropriately.

Barbie and Her Markers
by Lisa Burch

When Barbie finishes her school assignments, she loves to draw with her many colorful markers. She has learned that it is important to take care of her markers so they last a long time. When she is getting ready to draw, she puts the marker cap on the opposite end of the marker so she won't lose it. She is always careful to draw only on the paper so her desk and body stay clean. When she is finished with a marker, she carefully puts the cap back on.

Barbie wants every girl and boy to take good care of their markers. She has learned that it is important to have markers with caps so her favorite colors don't dry up.

Barbie wants you to remember these three things:

1. Put the cap on the end of your marker before you draw.

2. Be careful to only draw on the paper.

3. Put the cap back on the marker when you are finished.

Try your best to remember these three things so you can draw just like Barbie!!

Luke

To avoid completing assignments, Luke, a 10-year-old boy with Asperger Syndrome, repeatedly breaks his pencils and destroys erasers. Luke has a special interest in the television game show *Family Feud*, hosted by Louie Anderson. Luke enjoys playing the role of Louie Anderson and frequently plays the game with his younger brother and sister. This scenario and POWER CARD resulted in a decrease in the target behavior.

1. Keep your pencil in one piece.
2. Make sure your pencil always has a sharp point and a good eraser.
3. Be responsible for keeping track of your pencil.

Louie Anderson and His Pencil
by Rachele M. Hill

When getting ready to host Family Feud, *Louie Anderson uses a pencil to prepare cards with information about each of his contestants. He has a limited amount of time to do this and knows that it is important to use his pencil wisely. He likes to keep his pencil all in one piece with a sharp point and a good eraser. He also keeps track of his pencil so it doesn't get lost.*

Louie wants everyone to know how important it is to have a pencil that is long, sharp, and neat. Louie knows students in school need to have a good pencil every day. Louie is always proud of students who are responsible for their long, sharp, and neat pencils.

Louie Anderson wants you to remember these three things:

1. *Keep your pencil in one piece.*

2. *Make sure your pencil always has a sharp point and a good eraser.*

3. *Be responsible for keeping track of your pencil.*

Try your best to remember these things and you will always be a winner in the classroom.

1. Wash your hands after you go to the bathroom.
2. Always use soap.
3. Dry your hands completely.

Jennifer

Jennifer is a second-grade student in a regular education classroom, who has a medical diagnosis of Asperger Syndrome. She has acquired many social skills, such as initiating a conversation and introducing visitors to the class, and she independently uses the school restroom. However, Jennifer consistently forgets to wash her hands after using the toilet.

Jennifer's teacher wrote the following scenario and POWER CARD featuring Angelica from Jennifer's favorite cartoon, *The Rugrats*, to remind her to wash her hands. An enlarged copy of Jennifer's POWER CARD was placed in the restroom to remind all the students of the proper steps to handwashing.

Angelica Says, "Wash Those Hands"
by Rachele M. Hill

Angelica knows how important it is to keep her hands clean. She does not want to catch any yucky germs from "those babies!" Germs can cause coughing, sneezing, and runny noses. Angelica definitely does not want to catch a cold! She washes her hands often and always after using the bathroom. She knows that washing her hands helps avoid catching a cold.

Angelica wants you to have clean hands, too. She wants you to remember to wash your hands often and every time after you go to the bathroom.

Angelica wants you to remember these three things:

1. Wash your hands after you go to the bathroom.

2. Always use soap.

3. Dry your hands completely.

Angelica can be very bossy, but she does have manners when it comes to having clean hands. Angelica says, "Please wash your hands!"

Kelly

Kelly is a 15-year-old with a diagnosis of autism. She does not enjoy riding the school bus and often complains about the noisy brakes. She also becomes distressed when getting on and off the bus. Kelly enjoys watching *The Rugrats* on television after school. After she was introduced to the Power Card Strategy, Kelly's teachers and parents saw an improvement in Kelly's behavior on the bus and less apprehension about the bus rides to and from school.

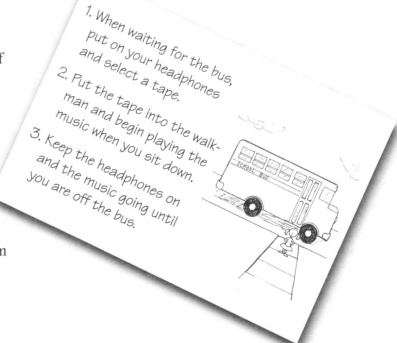

1. When waiting for the bus, put on your headphones and select a tape.

2. Put the tape into the walk-man and begin playing the music when you sit down.

3. Keep the headphones on and the music going until you are off the bus.

Angelica and the School Bus
by Kitty Flinn

Angelica can often be seen riding the school bus. She enjoys going to school and knows that riding the bus means getting a break from "those babies." What Angelica doesn't like about the bus are the noisy brakes, but she found a solution to the problem. Angelica now wears headphones on the bus and listens to her favorite music all the way to school and back home again.

Just like Angelica, students everywhere can wear headphones on the bus. It is lots of fun to listen to your favorite music or stories on the bus. Many children have found that when they enjoy the bus ride, it makes it easier to get on and off the bus.

Angelica would like for you to remember these three things:

1. When waiting for the bus, put on your headphones and select a tape.

2. Put the tape into the walkman and begin playing the music when you sit down.

3. Keep the headphones on and the music going until you are off the bus.

Angelica is thrilled when students take her advice and wear headphones on the bus!

1. Smile and put out your right hand and shake the other person's right hand.

2. Introduce yourself and ask the person how they are.

3. Practice greetings with your friends and teachers.

Kimberly

Kimberly, an 11-year-old girl with autism, hugs everyone she sees. As she is getting older, this behavior is appearing more and more inappropriate and her parents are becoming increasingly concerned about it. They have tried a variety of interventions, but Kimberly continues to insist that she hug each and every person she encounters. Kimberly loves country music singers, particularly Shania Twain. Using the Power Card Strategy, Kimberly's parents were able to teach their daughter a more appropriate greeting.

Photographer: George Holz.
Reprinted courtesy of Mercury Records.

Shania Twain Greets Her Fans
by Kitty Flinn

Shania Twain meets hundreds of people each year. After her concerts, she spends time with her fans, greeting them and autographing pictures. She used to hug all the people she met and then realized that this is not the only way, or the best way, to greet somebody she is meeting for the first time. Some people do not like to be hugged, especially by someone they are meeting for the first time. Just like Shania, it is important for everybody to learn to greet appropriately.

Shania is anxious to share these three key points that she has learned about greeting people:

1. Smile and put out your right hand and shake the other person's right hand.

2. Introduce yourself and ask the person how they are.

3. Practice greetings with your friends and teachers.

Following these steps will help you greet people just like Shania!!

John

John, an eight-year-old boy with autism, does not go to the bathroom unless someone reminds him. As a result, he sometimes wets his pants and then becomes angry with his mother or teacher because they did not remind him to go to the bathroom. John's favorite cartoon character is Superman, and he enjoys pretending that he is Superman or Clark Kent. The following scenario and POWER CARD were introduced to John to encourage him to use the bathroom independently.

1. When you are at home, don't wait for someone to ask if you need to go to the bathroom. Just go when you need to go.

2. When you are at school, tell your teacher that you need to go to the bathroom. Try and go every time there is a scheduled break, even if you don't feel you need to.

3. If you are away from home, tell an adult you are with that you need to use the bathroom and have them show you where it is located.

Superman and the Bathroom
by Kitty Flinn

During his many flights to help people in need, Superman has found it necessary to stop and use the bathroom once in a while. He knows it is important to go when he needs to, and he doesn't wait for someone to ask him if he has to go. He knows that it is important for superheroes to take care of their bathroom needs on their own.

Superman would like for you to consider these three facts:

1. *When you are at home, don't wait for someone to ask if you need to go to the bathroom. Just go when you need to go.*

2. *When you are at school, tell your teacher that you need to go to the bathroom. Try and go every time there is a scheduled break, even if you don't feel you need to.*

3. *If you are away from home, tell an adult you are with that you need to use the bathroom and have them show you where it is located.*

Superman is proud of young men who can take care of their own bathroom needs.

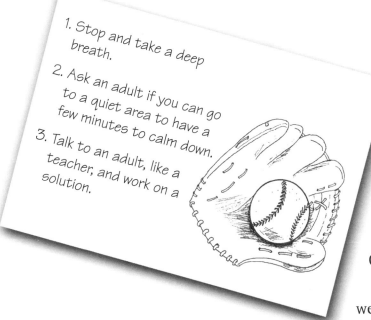

1. Stop and take a deep breath.

2. Ask an adult if you can go to a quiet area to have a few minutes to calm down.

3. Talk to an adult, like a teacher, and work on a solution.

Tommy

Tommy is a nine-year-old boy with Asperger Syndrome. He is in a fourth-grade classroom most of the day but sometimes becomes frustrated when he has difficulty completing his work. At times, he falls to the ground kicking and screaming and has difficulty regaining his composure. These tantrums can last up to 45 minutes. Tommy loves baseball, particularly his hero, Cal Ripken.

The following scenario and POWER CARD were introduced to Tommy in an attempt to reduce his tantrums.

How Cal Ripken Handles Frustration
by Kitty Flinn

Cal Ripken is one of the best baseball players of all times. He has enjoyed playing for the Baltimore Orioles for 15 years. Cal understands that it is very important to work hard and stay focused on and off the field. However, there are times when Cal gets frustrated and feels like falling to the ground screaming. He realizes that this would be inappropriate. He knows that if he behaved this way, the umpire would throw him out of the game.

Cal wants everyone to know how important it is to handle frustrations appropriately. He began working on controlling his temper when he was in elementary school and has advice for all boys who feel frustrated.

The next time you begin to feel a little frustrated, try doing the following three things that helped Cal:

1. Stop and take a deep breath.

2. Ask an adult if you can go to a quiet area to have a few minutes to calm down.

3. Talk to an adult, like a teacher, and work on a solution.

Work on these rules and you will score a homerun in the classroom!

Charlie

Charlie is a seventh grader with Asperger Syndrome. He has a great deal of trouble with handwriting. Not only is his handwriting difficult to read, but Charlie becomes extremely agitated while taking notes in his classes. As a result, he often interrupts the teacher by blurting out statements like "Slow down!" or "You're talking so fast I can't keep up!" Charlie is interesting in Pokémon™ trading cards and enjoys discussing the Pokémon characters with his classmates. The following scenario and POWER CARD were created to help Charlie accept alternatives to taking handwritten notes in class.

1. When his friend Ash is around, Brock dictates his words and Ash writes down every exciting detail.

2. Sometimes Ash puts a piece of carbon paper behind a letter he is writing. That way a copy is automatically made for Brock.

3. Brock also uses the computer to type his stories. He isn't very fast yet but that doesn't matter. Brock knows that the more he types, the faster he gets.

Brock's Handwriting
by Carla Huhtanen

Writing is not an easy skill for many people. Many of our most admired professionals, such as doctors, lawyers, or even teachers, have problems with handwriting. Even Brock has difficulty putting legible letters on paper. Every week when he is away from home finding new Pokémon, he writes to his brothers and sisters. He is concerned that his family will not be able to enjoy reading about the many wonderful adventures he is experiencing around the world.

Because of his concerns, Brock came up with three terrific solutions.

1. When his friend Ash is around, Brock dictates his words and Ash writes down every exciting detail.

2. Sometimes Ash puts a piece of carbon paper behind a letter he is writing. That way a copy is automatically made for Brock.

3. Brock also uses the computer to type his stories. He isn't very fast yet but that doesn't matter. Brock knows that the more he types, the faster he gets.

Just like Brock, other kids who have problems with handwriting can learn strategies to keep in touch with family and friends. Follow Brock's suggestions and you too can say what you want to say in writing!

1. Say "I want pink shoes" to your teacher.

2. Have a quiet mouth (no giggling).

3. Look at your shoes or your Minnie Card to remember the rule.

From *Picture Communication Symbols* ©1981-1999 used with permission from Mayer-Johnson Inc., P.O. Box 1579, Solana Beach, CA 92075, 858/550-0084.

Minnie

Minnie is a seven-year-old with autism. She exhibits many of the characteristics of autism, including avoiding eye contact, echolalia, and self-stimulatory behavior such as rocking, flapping and attachment to unusual objects. In addition, she spends much of the time laughing at nothing in particular. The high-pitched sound of her giggles is of particular concern to her classroom teacher. Minnie does not read social cues, including the "teacher look," and responds to such a look by giggling even louder. A reinforcement inventory revealed that Minnie has few interests outside of self-stimulatory behaviors, giggling and her Minnie Mouse doll.

Minnie is very attached to her Minnie Mouse doll and insists on carrying it with her most of the time. She constantly points to the doll's pink shoes stating the words "pink shoes." This behavior occurs up to 100 times in a school day.

The classroom teacher wrote the following scenario and POWER CARD in conjunction with a behavior plan in hopes of reducing Minnie's giggling at school. Since Minnie has not learned to read, her POWER CARD is two-sided with a picture of Minnie Mouse's pink shoes on one side and a quiet mouth icon on the reverse side.

Minnie Mouse and the Pink Shoes
by Elisa Gagnon

Minnie Mouse loves to wear her pink shoes. She thinks her pink shoes are the most beautiful shoes in the world. Sometimes Mickey Mouse says to her, "Minnie, I just love your shoes." Just like Minnie Mouse, girls with quiet mouths at school can wear pink shoes. To get pink shoes, girls need to say, "I want pink shoes" to their teacher.

It is important to have a quiet mouth at school. It is okay to talk in a quiet voice but giggling all the time is not okay.

Minnie Mouse wants all girls who love pink shoes to remember these three things:

1. Say "I want pink shoes" to your teacher.

2. Have a quiet mouth (no giggling).

3. Look at your shoes or your Minnie Card to remember the rule.

Remember to have a quiet mouth and you can have pink shoes just like Minnie!*

*This scenario was more effective in a booklet form with illustrations.

Sam

Sam is a highly intelligent sixth-grade student with a diagnosis of Asperger Syndrome. Sam hopes one day to attend Harvard and often speaks of this plan to anyone willing to listen. But even though Sam is intelligent, he has developed few organizational strategies. Specifically, he doesn't ask questions about course requirements and therefore often fails to turn in assignments on time. The following scenario and POWER CARD were introduced to Sam by his mother to provide him with organizational strategies.

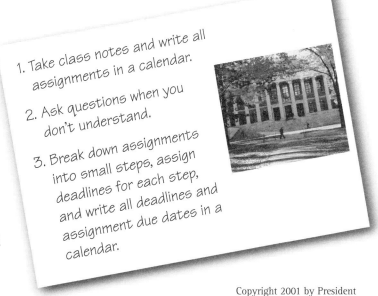

1. Take class notes and write all assignments in a calendar.

2. Ask questions when you don't understand.

3. Break down assignments into small steps, assign deadlines for each step, and write all deadlines and assignment due dates in a calendar.

A Harvard Student
by Becky Heinrichs

Dave is proud to be a student at Harvard. He spent many hours studying throughout middle school and high school so he could achieve his dream. He always had difficulty with organization and relied on his mother to keep track of course requirements, paperwork, and due dates. When Dave got to Harvard, he realized that he was having difficulty with organization. He scheduled a meeting with his English professor and explained his problems to him and received the following advice:

1. Take class notes and write all assignments in a calendar.

2. Ask questions when you don't understand.

3. Break down assignments into small steps, assign deadlines for each step, and write all deadlines and assignment due dates in a calendar.

You do not have to wait to get to Harvard to practice these three steps. Dave now knows that he would have enjoyed middle school and high school much more if he would have tried these things earlier.

Greg

Greg is an 11-year-old boy with autism. He is prompt-dependent throughout the school day, looking to his teacher or paraprofessionals to provide him with every instruction. Greg is interested in cartoon videos and his parents report that his favorite video is *Charlotte's Web*. The following scenario and POWER CARD were developed to address Greg's prompt dependency.

Wilbur Takes Charge
by Cindy Van Horn

Charlotte the spider loves her best friend, Wilbur the pig. Lately, Charlotte has been frustrated with Wilbur because he will not do anything unless she tells him what to do. Wilbur will not eat unless Charlotte tells him it is time to eat. Wilbur will not clean his pigpen unless Charlotte tells him to clean it. In fact, Wilbur won't even play with the other pigs unless Charlotte tells him it's time to play. Charlotte is tired! She knows Wilbur will be a happier pig if he asks for help instead of always having to be told what to do.

Just like Wilbur, it is important for all boys at school to be independent. It is important to do your work on your own without someone telling you what to do. If you don't know what to do, it is OK to ask for help. For example, boys can go through the lunch line by themselves without someone telling them every step they need to take. Of course, boys can always ask for help if they need it. Charlotte has decided she is going to wait for Wilbur to ask for help instead of always telling him what to do. She wants Wilbur to take charge!

Just remember Charlotte's three rules for taking charge:

1. If you are not sure what to do, check your schedule.

2. Don't wait for someone to tell you what to do. Just do it!!

3. If you need help say, "I need help."

Remember these three things and you can take charge just like Wilbur!

Chapter 5

Results of Classroom Studies Using the Power Card Strategy

with Brenda Smith Myles, Katharine Keeling and Cindy Van Horn

Research on techniques used with children and youth with Asperger Syndrome and autism is often not published until the strategies have been implemented for several years. For example, Carol Gray's social stories (1995) were used in schools and homes for more than five years before any research on their effectiveness appeared in peer-refereed journals. The Power Card Strategy is not different in this regard. Despite positive results in the classroom, the findings have not yet been widely disseminated.

Some of the most socially valid research in autism and Asperger Syndrome comes from teachers who implement strategies and measure their impact on students. These teacher-researchers often are the best judges of the effectiveness of teaching methods for their students. What follows are two syntheses of classroom-based research conducted using the Power Card Strategy.

> *Some of the most socially valid research in autism and Asperger Syndrome comes from teachers who implement strategies and measure their impact on students.*

Nancy

At the time of this study, Nancy was a nine-year-old girl diagnosed with autism. She participated in fourth-grade general education activities with the aid of a paraprofessional and received support from a resource room teacher. Her Individualized Education Plan (IEP) targeted the following areas: speech/language, reading, math and written language.

Despite average intelligence, Nancy had academic problems. Although she could decode and identify words at her grade level, her reading comprehension was only at the second-grade level. Writing was also a challenge for her, particularly when it came to writing complete sentences using appropriate grammar and punctuation. Math was considered a strength. She was fluent in basic facts, and geometry was a relative strength. Nancy received special education services 90 minutes a day five times per week and speech-language therapy for 60 minutes per week.

The remainder of her school day was spent with her general education fourth-grade class.

Nancy demonstrated behaviors that her general and special education peers considered inappropriate when she was placed in a situation that she could not control, such as when she lost a game. The following is a brief example of one situation — her peers reported many similar instances.

A popular activity for fourth graders is the game Four Square, which involves a ball and a large square divided into four sections. Four players play at once, with one person in each square. To play, one person passes the ball to someone else. That person has to let it bounce before he or she hits the ball to another player. If the ball is hit out of the square, the player is out of the game. When Nancy hit the ball out of the square while playing this game, she tried to verbally defend her right to stay in the game even as the other children explained the rules. When required to leave the game area, Nancy began to whine, and escalated to screaming. Because of such behavior, her peers did not want to play with her.

To help Nancy learn other ways to act or things to say when she lost a game, her teacher and student teacher decided to use the Power Card Strategy, which they personalized for Nancy using her special interest: The Powerpuff Girls. At school Nancy spent time each day drawing the cartoon characters, singing the theme song, discussing the cartoon with peers and reciting cartoon episodes she had seen in the past. The following script was developed that featured pictures of the Powerpuff Girls.

1. Games should be fun for everyone.

2. If you win a game, you can: smile, give a high five, or say, "yea!"

3. If you lose a game you can: take a deep breath, say, "good job" to the winner, or say, "maybe next time."

Illustration by Katharine Keeling

The Powerpuff Girls Play a Game

The Powerpuff Girls like to play games. Sometimes they win the game. When they win games the Powerpuff Girls feel happy. They might smile, give each other a high five or say "yea!" But sometimes they lose the game. When they lose games, the Powerpuff Girls might not feel happy. They might take a deep breath, say "good job" to the winner or say, "maybe next time."

The Powerpuff Girls want everyone to have fun playing games. They want you to remember these three things when playing games the Powerpuff way:

1. Games should be fun for everyone.

2. If you win a game you can: smile, give a high five, or say, "yea!"

3. If you lose a game you can: Take a deep breath, say, "good job" to your friend or say, "maybe next time."

A laminated POWER CARD with the steps to play a game like the Powerpuff Girls was also developed. The Power Card Strategy was implemented using three types of games: a gross-motor game (bowling), a board game (Labyrinth Jr.), and a card game (Go Fish). Each game was played daily. The strategy was systematically implemented in one game type at a time using a multiple-baseline-across-settings design.

Nancy read the entire script aloud at the beginning of the first three sessions. The script was always visible during the playing and the scoring of the gross-motor game. Following this introduction (after Session 3), Nancy was allowed to choose either the "long" or "short" version (that is, either the script or the POWER CARD). Nancy chose to read only the POWER CARD for every subsequent session. The POWER CARD continued to be visible to Nancy during the games.

When the POWER CARD was introduced during the other two games, the same procedure was followed. During the second week of the study, Nancy began adding her own positive behaviors to those listed on the POWER CARD. For example, after reading the

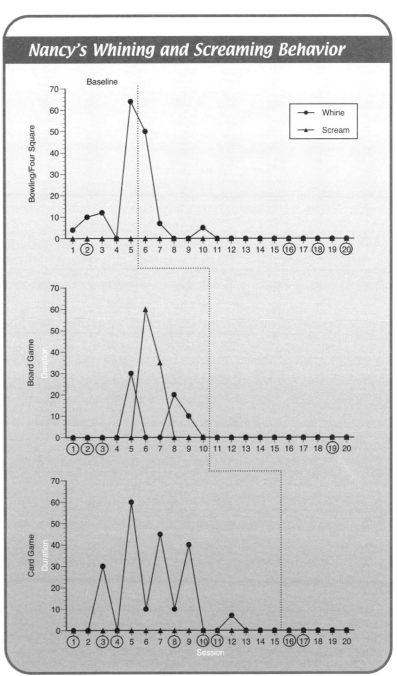

three printed behaviors on the card, she commented to her teacher, "You could say, 'Oh well.'" This statement was then added to the POWER CARD. From that point, Nancy continually updated the list.

As shown in the graph on page 53, Nancy's whining and screaming behaviors decreased once the Power Card Strategy was introduced. For example, when this technique was used in the gross-motor game, Nancy used appropriate language when she lost a game. She did not use this language in the other two games. However, when the Power Card Strategy was used in the gross-motor game and board game, she used her Powerpuff Girls' words when she lost these games as well as when she lost the card game. No instances of negative behavior were recorded after the Power Card Strategy was introduced in the second condition.

Perhaps most exciting were reports from other teachers who taught Nancy. Anecdotal reports of generalization occurred during the study. For example, Mr. Brothers, her general education teacher, had expressed several times in the past that Nancy had trouble controlling her actions when she lost educational games in class. He recently indicated that Nancy had generalized the Power Card Strategy in his classroom. Specifically, the class was playing a "spelling bee" type game one day using the states and their capitals instead of spelling words. Nancy was very excited about playing because she knew almost all the states and their capitals. As the game progressed, Nancy and another student were competing for the championship. Mr. Brothers reported that during the "spelling bee" he worried about an outburst from Nancy if she did not win. However, Nancy won the game and did not scream with excitement. Moreover, when the student who came in second began to get upset, Nancy turned to her and said, "You can take a deep breath, or say 'maybe next time.'" In other words, Nancy used her knowledge of how to win and lose games and shared it with her peer.

Nancy's speech-language pathologist also saw the Power Card Strategy work in one of her sessions with Nancy and three other students, who played a communication game. According to the rules of the game, once a player gave an inaccurate response, she was eliminated from the game. Nancy was eliminated on her first turn. When she began to whine, the speech-language pathologist mentioned the Power Card Strategy. Nancy's behavior immediately changed, and she watched the remainder of the game quietly.

Nancy's teacher reported that after the first week of the study, Nancy began to the use the Power Card Strategy at recess. When she lost a Four Square or Freeze Tag game, she would say the positive responses printed on the POWER CARD. Nancy's teacher reported that it appeared that peers were asking Nancy to play games with them more often because she was a "good sport."

Scott

Scott was an 11-year-old boy diagnosed with Asperger Syndrome. Scott had above average intelligence but had difficulty with written language, organizational skills, attention to task, and social skills. Scott followed the fifth-grade curriculum, but it was modified so he could be successful. His IEP indicated that his placement was in a general education fifth-grade classroom.

The behavior that concerned Scott's teachers and parents the most was noncompliance. That is, when Scott was asked or told to do something that he did not want to do, he would (a) verbally refuse; (b) begin to talk about a special interest; and (c) escalate to a tantrum that could include yelling, crying, throwing things, kicking, shoving furniture, and cursing. These behaviors were considered so severe that he had to complete most of his work in a resource room setting.

Scott's favorite activities were playing SEGA games and drawing "Gerball" cards and handing them out to peers. The latter was considered an obsession that distracted Scott from completing his work and was, therefore, limited to lunch and recess.

To help Scott learn new strategies to better cope with completing non-preferred activities, the Power Card Strategy was introduced using his favorite cartoon characters, Ed, Edd n Eddy. A Power Card script was written explaining what Ed, Edd n Eddy do when they become angry about having to do something they do not want to do.

Ed, Edd n Eddy Keep Their Cool

Ed, Edd n Eddy are three friends who love to eat jawbreakers and play SEGA games. Most of the time, Ed, Edd n Eddy earn jawbreakers or SEGA time by doing their schoolwork. Sometimes they have to do schoolwork that they don't like to do. This makes them angry. In the past when they got angry, they yelled, which got them into trouble. But they didn't like getting in trouble because not only did they not get jawbreakers or time to play SEGA, they also didn't get their work done, which made them and their

When I feel I am getting angry, I can:

1. Count to 10 in my head and tell the adult I would like to negotiate.

2. Write my feelings in my special journal while the adult gives me my space.

3. Tell the adult I need a break. I can get a drink of water and chill until I am ready to work again.

Illustration by Katharine Keeling

teacher sad. If they didn't get their work done, it became homework, and they did not like that as they wanted to do other things when they got home. So they decided to come up with some other things to do when they felt themselves getting angry.

Ed, Edd n Eddy found that these three things helped them keep their cool when they felt themselves getting angry:

1. *Count to 10 in their head and tell the adult they would like to negotiate.*

2. *Write their feelings in their special journal while the adult gives them their space.*

3. *Tell the adult they need a break. They can get a drink of water and chill until they are ready to work again.*

Remember, when you feel yourself getting angry, try one of the three things Ed, Edd n Eddy do to calm down. That way, you will feel better, get your work done, and still have time to play SEGA!

The POWER CARD, the size of a trading card, summarized what Scott could do to be like Ed, Edd n Eddy when he became angry. A POWER CARD was placed on his desk in both his general education classroom and the resource room. It read:

When I feel I am getting angry, I can:

1. Count to 10 in my head and tell the adult I would like to negotiate.

2. Write my feelings in my special journal while the adult gives me my space.

3. Tell the adult I need a break. I can get a drink of water and chill until I am ready to work again.

The table on the following page overviews Scott's tantrumming before the Power Card Strategy was used (baseline) and after it was introduced. During baseline, Scott did not have a tantrum every day, but when it did occur, it caused him to be off-task for a significant amount of time. His screaming also disrupted other students and staff because it could be heard throughout the building. In fact, younger students were frightened of Scott's screaming.

Scott's Tantrum Behavior Before and After the Power Card Strategy Was Introduced			
Day		**Number of Tantrums**	**Duration of Tantrums**
BASELINE	Day 1	1	35 minutes
	Day 2	0	—
	Day 3	1	45 minutes
	Day 4	0	—
	Day 5	0	—
	Day 6	0	—
INTERVENTION	Day 7	1	10 minutes
	Day 8	2	30 seconds; 60 seconds
	Day 9	1	15 seconds
	Day 10	0	—
	Day 11	2	5 minutes; 10 minutes
	Day 12	0	—
	Day 13	0	—
	Day 14	0	—

During the intervention Scott and his teacher read the Power Card script each morning. They also reviewed and practiced the options written on the POWER CARD. As reinforcement for practicing the three behaviors, he watched 10 minutes of an *Ed, Edd n Eddy* program that had been videotaped for him.

Although the number of tantrums did not decrease when the strategy was introduced, a significant decrease was seen in the length of his tantrums (see the table above). His favorite option was to write in his special journal. He wrote why he was angry and listed everything that he was thinking when he began to get upset. Scott's teacher was hopeful that his tantrums would continue to decrease in number and duration.

Summary

These two cases illustrate the potential impact of the Power Card Strategy. Due to its versatility and focus on the child's special interest, this technique can be easily used in the classroom and at home. The Power Card Strategy is both an instructional and interpretative strategy (see Myles & Southwick, 1998). It teaches the child or youth what she is supposed to do and helps her better understand her world.

American Psychiatric Association. (2000). *Diagnostic and statistical manual of mental disorders* (4th ed.-text rev.). Washington, DC: Author.

Asperger, H. (1944). Die 'Autistichen Psychopathern' in Kindersalter. *Archiv für Psychiatrie und Nervenkrankheiten, 117,* 76-136.

Baker, J. (in press). *Social skills training: Practical solutions for students with Asperger Syndrome, high-functioning autism, and related social communication disorders.* Shawnee Mission, KS: AAPC.

Baker, M. (2000). Incorporating the thematic ritualistic behaviors of children with autism into games: Increasing social play interactions with siblings. *Journal of Positive Behavior Interventions, 2,* 66-84.

Baker, M., Koegel, R., & Koegel, L. K. (1998). Increasing the social behavior of young children with autism using their obsessive interests. *Journal of the Association for Persons with Severe Handicaps, 23(4),* 300-309.

Barnhill, G., Hagiwara, R., Myles, B. S., & Simpson, R. L. (2000). Asperger Syndrome: A study of the cognitive profiles of 37 children and adolescents. *Focus on Autism and Other Developmental Disabilities, 15,* 146-153.

Baron-Cohen, S. (1988). An assessment of violence in a young man with Asperger's Syndrome. *Journal of Child Psychology and Psychiatry, 29,* 351-360.

Bieber, J. (Producer). (1994). *Learning disabilities and social skills with Richard LaVoie: Last one picked ... first one picked on.* Washington, DC: Public Broadcasting Service.

Bock, M. A. (1994). Acquisition, maintenance, and generalization of a categorization strategy by children with autism. *Journal of Autism and Developmental Disorders, 24,* 39-51.

Bock, M. A. (1999). Sorting laundry: Categorization strategy application to an authentic learning activity by children with autism. *Focus on Autism and Other Developmental Disabilities, 14,* 220-230.

Carnine, D. (1991). Direct instruction applied to mathematics in a general education classroom. In J. Lloyd, N. Singh, & A. Repp (Eds.), *The regular education initiative: Alternative perspectives on concepts, issues, and models* (pp. 163-175). Sycamore, IL: Sycamore.

Charlop-Christy, M., & Haynes, L. (1998). Using objects of obsession as token reinforcers for children with autism. *Journal of Autism and Developmental Disorders, 28,* 189-197.

Dunlap, G., Foster-Johnson, L., Clarke, S., Kern, L., & Childs, K. E. (1995). Modifying activities to produce functional outcomes: Effects on the problem behaviors of students with disabilities. *Journal of the Association for Persons with Severe Handicaps, 20,* 248-258.

Dunn, W., Myles, B. S., & Orr, S. (in press). Sensory processing issues in Asperger Syndrome. *The American Journal of Occupational Therapy.*

Durand, V. M., & Crimmins, D. (1992). *Motivation assessment scale.* Topeka, KS: Monaco & Associates.

Ehlers, S., Nyden, A., Gillberg, C., Sandberg, A. D., Dahlgren, S., Hjelmquist, E., & Oden, A. (1997). Asperger Syndrome, autism and attention deficit disorders: A comparative study of cognitive profiles of 120 children. *Journal of Child Psychology and Psychiatry and Allied Disciplines, 38,* 207-217.

Freeman, S., & Dake, L. (1997). *Teach me language: A language manual for children with autism, Asperger's Syndrome, and related developmental disabilities.* Langley, BC, Canada: SKF Books.

Frith, U. (1991). *Autism and Asperger Syndrome.* Cambridge, UK: Cambridge University Press.

Gagnon, E., & Myles, B. S. (1999). *This Is Asperger Syndrome.* Shawnee Mission, KS: AAPC.

Gray, C. A. (1995). Teaching children with autism to "read" social situations. In K. A. Quill (Ed.), *Teaching children with autism: Strategies to enhance communication and socialization* (pp. 219-241). Albany, NY: Delmar.

Hinton, M., & Kern, L. (1999). Increasing homework completion by incorporating student interests. *Journal of Positive Behavior Interventions, 1,* 231-234, 241.

Hodgdon, L. A. (1995). *Visual strategies for improving communication: Practical supports for school and home.* Troy, MI: Quirk Roberts.

Howlin, P. (1998). *Children with autism and Asperger Syndrome: A guide for practitioners and careers.* New York: John Wiley and Sons.

Howlin, P., Baron-Cohen, S., & Hadwin, J. (1999). *Teaching children with autism to mind-read: A practical guide.* New York: John Wiley & Sons.

Kamps, D. M., Dugan, E. P., Leonard, B. R., & Carta, J. J. (1990). *Peer tutoring and small group instruction.* Kansas City: University of Kansas, Bureau of Child Research, Juniper Garden's Children's Project.

Kanner, L. (1943). Autistic disturbances of affective content. *The Nervous Child, 2,* 217-250.

Kern, L., Dunlap, G., Clarke, S., & Childs, K. (1994). Student-assisted functional assessment interview. *Diagnostique, 19*(2-3), 29-39.

Leaf, R., & McEachin, J. (1999). *A work in progress: Behavior management strategies and a curriculum for intensive behavioral treatment of autism.* New York: DRL Books.

Lovaas, I. O. (1987). Behavioral treatment and normal educational and intellectual functioning in young autistic children. *Journal of Consulting and Clinical Psychology, 55,* 3-9.

Mayer-Johnson, R. (1981). *The picture communication symbols book.* Solana Beach, CA: Author.

McGee, G. G., Almeida, M. C., Sulzer-Azaroff, B., & Feldman, R. S. (1992). Promoting reciprocal social interactions via peer incidental teaching. *Journal of Applied Behavior Analysis, 25,* 117-126

McGee, G. G., Krantz, P. J., & McClannahan, L. E. (1985). Facilitative effects of incidental teaching on preposition use by autistic children. *Journal of Applied Behavior Analysis, 18,* 17-31.

Mercier, C., Mottron, L., & Belleville, S. (2000). Psychosocial study on restricted interests in high-functioning persons with pervasive developmental disorders. *Autism, 4*(4), 496-425.

Myles, B. S., & Simpson, R. L. (1998). *Asperger Syndrome: A guide for educators and parents.* Austin, TX: Pro-Ed.

Myles, B. S., & Simpson, R. L. (2001). Understanding the hidden curriculum: An essential social skill for children and youth with Asperger Syndrome. *Intervention in School and Clinic, 36*(5), 279-286.

Myles, B. S., & Southwick, J. (1999). *Asperger syndrome and difficult moments: Practical solutions for tantrums, rage, and meltdowns.* Shawnee Mission, KS: AAPC.

Odom, S. L., & McConnell, S. R. (1997). *Play time/social time: Organizing your classroom to build interaction skills.* Minneapolis: University of Minnesota, Institute on Community Integration.

Olly, J. G. (1992). Autism: Historical overview, definition and characteristics. In D. Berkell (Ed.), *Autism: Identification, education and treatment* (pp. 3-20). Hillsdale, NJ: Erlbaum.

Paramount Pictures. (1995). *Forrest Gump.* Hollywood: Authors.

Quill, K. (2000). *DO-WATCH-LISTEN-SAY: Social and communication intervention for children with autism.* Baltimore, MD: Paul H. Brookes.

Quill, K. (1995). *Teaching children with autism: Strategies to enhance communication and socialization.* New York: Delmar.

Quinn, C., Swaggart, B. L., & Myles, B. S. (1994). Implementing cognitive behavior management programs for persons with autism: Guidelines for practitioners. *Focus on Autistic Behavior, 9(4)*, 1-13.

Savner, J. L., & Myles, B. S. (2000). *Making visual supports work in the home and community: Strategies for individuals with autism and Asperger Syndrome.* Shawnee Mission, KS: AAPC.

Schopler, E., & Mesibov, G. B. (1995). Introduction to learning and cognition in autism. In E. Schopler & G. B. Mesibov (Eds.), *Learning and cognition in autism* (pp. 3-11). New York: Plenum.

Simpson, R. L., & Myles, B. S. (1998). *Educating children and youth with autism*: *Strategies for effective practice.* Austin, TX: Pro-Ed.

Simpson, R. L., & Myles, B. S. (1990). A clinical/prescriptive method for use with students with autism. *Focus on Autistic Behavior, 4(6)*, 1-15.

Snyder-McLean, L. K., Solomonson, B., McLean, J. E., & Sack, S. (1984). Structuring joint action routines: A strategy for facilitating communication and language development in the classroom. *Seminars in Speech and Language, 5*, 213-228.

Sugai, G., & White, W. J. (1986). Effects of using object self-stimulation as a reinforcer on the prevocational work rates of an autistic child. *Journal of Autism and Developmental Disorders, 16,* 459-470.

Swaggart, B., Gagnon, E., Bock, S., Earles, T., Quinn, C., Myles, B. S., & Simpson, R. L. (1995). Using social stories to teach social and behavioral skills to children with autism. *Focus on Autistic Behavior, 10,* 1-16.

Williams, M. S., & Shellenberger, S. (1996). *How does your engine run? A leader's guide to the alert program for self-regulation.* Albuquerque, NM: TherapyWorks, Inc.

Wilson, C. C. (1993). *Room 14: A social language program.* East Moline, IL: LinguiSystems.

Wing, L. (1981). Asperger's Syndrome: A clinical account. *Psychological Medicine, 11,* 115-129.